D0734841

The Snark Handbook

PARENTING EDITION

MORNING SICKNESS, POTTY TRAINING, REBELLIOUS TEENS, AND OTHER JOYS

LAWRENCE DORFMAN

Skyhorse Publishing

Skyhorse Publishing books may be purchased in bulk at special discounts for sales promotion, corporate gifts, fund-raising, or educational purposes. Special editions can also be created to specifications. For details, contact the Special Sales Department, Skyhorse Publishing, 307 West 36th Street, 11th Floor, New York, NY 10018 or info@skyhorsepublishing.com.

Skyhorse® and Skyhorse Publishing® are registered trademarks of Skyhorse Publishing, Inc.®, a Delaware corporation.

Visit our website at www.skyhorsepublishing.com.

10 9 8 7 6 5 4 3 2 1

Library of Congress Cataloging-in-Publication Data is available on file.

ISBN: 978-1-62087-784-5

Printed in China

CONTENTS

Introduction

WELL, THIS TIME I just might be on shaky ground . . .

Okay, let's recap.

This is the seventh time I've gone back to the *Snark* well . . . seems kinda endless, no?

Over the previous books, we explored the art of verbal sparring and learned how to raise the level of insult. We moved ever so gently into the hot and steamy world of sex and lived to tell the tale. We discovered ways to retain one's sanity during the holidays and come out the other end in *basically* one piece. We traversed the political landscape in an election year when the big decision was whom to vote against instead of whom to vote for, and we went semi-hard at the verbal flotsam and jetsam known in literary circles as "clichés."

(Ya know???)

Now, dear reader, you hold in your hands *The Snark Handbook: Parenting Edition.*

What's that you say? Daring to go after that holiest of holy institutions, that bastion of reverence known as Motherhood and Fatherhood? (Often used with a capital M & F . . . also the initials for one of the better curse words.)

Hey, you might ask, "Is he crazy?" "Does he chance ticking off the entire world?" After all, every one of us is either a mother or father or daughter or son. Am I not, indeed, on "shaky ground?"

Nah.

Throughout the ages, the one constant in literature (too many to even attempt to list here . . . suffice it to say it's truly one of the seven plots that all great novels can boil down to), in music (from Al Jolson to Paul Simon to the Beatles),[1] in film (again, way too many for the intro—snarky lists later), in politics (a constant battleground for the definition of family), and finally, in life itself, has always been the love/hate relationship we have with our parents as well as with our kids. (Perhaps "hate" is too strong a word; let's just call it an "irritation.")

Yes, the great Snarkists of both past and contemporary times have always had pithy and biting things to say about children, moms, dads, in-laws, grandparents . . . and it's time they were collected in one easily accessible place.

Now, I know that the purists out there will be all up in my grill about how many of the snarks herein are not particularly biting. Are they truly "snarks?" Where's the vitriolic bile

---

[1]   Together AND solo.

we've come to know and love? Where are the cutting remarks and the pithy bon mots that can eviscerate and cut to the quick?

Snark . . . where's the beef?

Look, nobody wants to bite the hands that feed them. Many of us still have a lot of holidays to attend in the coming years.

This book is merely intended to remove some of the gloss from a highly touted institution.

Yes, for far too long, the public has trodden ever so softly where the notion of "family" reigned supreme . . . it's a PC world, and many still cling to the notions made famous and banal in shows like *Little House on the Prairie* and *The Waltons* . . . that no matter what, when all is said and done, the FAMILY will be there for you. Right.

This book will show that it is not so . . . that it may never have been so. That it's all been a dream used to sell us a Rockwell existence and kept us fat and happy. . . .

But use it wisely. Use it as relief from the angst your kids throw at you in their teenage years. Use it to shield yourself from the barbs thrown at you during any variety of tantrum. . . . And, to paraphrase the great philosopher and son, Elmer Fudd, a word of caution . . . be vewy, vewy careful.

They know all your secrets.

Motherhood

Mothers are all slightly insane.
—J. D. SALINGER, *THE CATCHER IN THE RYE*

Insanity is hereditary—you get it from your children.
—SAM LEVENSON

A MEN, BROTHER . . . AND I say that with all the love and respect I can muster.

Mothers ARE slightly insane. And I'm sure there are a number of you out there who would argue with the use of "slightly."

Well, let's face it . . . you'd have to be more than a little crazy to take the job in the first place . . . comes down to that whole "repeating the same behavior and expecting different results" cliché. Trite . . . but on the money.

From the excruciating pain of childbirth[2] . . . to those first cuts and bruises . . . on toward all the versions of "Mom,

---

[2] Complete hearsay

I've got something to tell you" . . . the JOB[3] is fraught with enough potholes and booby traps to demand combat pay . . . which they never get.

It was always so. In the beginning, God[4] first looked at Adam, realized that man could never handle the pain and suffering of child bearing and so created Eve . . . to the moment when Eve ate them out of house and home . . . to the point where they decided to start a family and began to raise Cain . . . it was always so.

Some say that Cain and Abel were further punishment for the whole apple thing . . . hard to argue with that theory.

But clearly there have been "issues" throughout the years. Take a look.

Well, knowledge is a fine thing, and mother Eve thought so; but she smarted so severely for hers, that most of her daughters have been afraid of it since.
—ABIGAIL ADAMS

++

---

[3]   "Calling" . . . "avocation" . . . "undertaking" . . . give it a name.
[4]   Just want to mention that I'm not getting into the whole "Creation vs. Evolution" silliness. No letters.

Mothers are fonder than fathers of their children because they are more certain they are their own.
—ARISTOTLE

✦✦✦

Nobody loves me but my mother, and she could be jivin' too.
—B. B. KING

✦✦

The most remarkable thing about my mother is that for thirty years she served the family nothing but leftovers. The original meal has never been found.
—CALVIN TRILLIN

✦✦✦

Think of stretch marks as pregnancy service stripes.
—JOYCE ARMOR

✦✦

I know how to do anything—I'm a mom.
—ROSEANNE BARR

◆◆◆

Simply having children does not make mothers.
—JOHN A. SHEDD

◆◆

My mother used to say that there are no strangers, only friends you haven't met yet. She's now in a maximum security twilight home in Australia.
—DAME EDNA EVERAGE

◆◆◆

I'm a mother with two small children, so I don't take as much crap as I used to.
—PAMELA ANDERSON

◆◆

My mother never saw the irony in calling me a
son-of-a-bitch.
—JACK NICHOLSON

✦✦✦

My mom said the only reason men are alive is for lawn care
and vehicle maintenance.
—TIM ALLEN

✦✦

When your mother asks, "Do you want a piece of advice?" it
is a mere formality. It doesn't matter if you answer yes or no.
You're going to get it anyway.
—ERMA BOMBECK

✦✦✦

A suburban mother's role is to deliver children obstetrically
once, and by car for ever after.
—PETER DE VRIES

✦✦

Being a mother isn't simply a matter of having children. To think that is as absurd as believing that having a piano makes one a musician.
—SYDNEY HARRIS

+++

The hand that rocks the cradle is the hand that rules the world.
—W. R. WALLACE

++

An ounce of mother is worth a ton of priest.
—SPANISH PROVERB

+++

(24/7) . . . once you sign on to be a mother, that's the only shift they offer.
—JODI PICOULT

++

When my kids become wild and unruly, I use a nice, safe playpen. When they're finished, I climb out.
—ERMA BOMBECK

+++

Worst Parenting Books of All Time

Last Child in the Woods: Outrunning a Bear
Secrets of the Baby Whisperer: Teaching Your Child to Say,
  "Huh, What's That Again?"
Our Babies, Ourselves: But Mostly, Ourselves
Confessions of a Slacker Mom: A Lesson in Three Pages
Fatherhood: On Twenty Minutes a Week

If evolution really works, how come mothers only have
two hands?
—MILTON BERLE

✦✦

There are only two things a child will share willingly:
communicable diseases and his mother's age.
—DR. BENJAMIN SPOCK

✦✦✦

The worst feature of a new baby is its mother's singing.
—KIN HUBBARD

✦✦

My mom was a garage sale person, save money. Come on in to the garage sale, you might find a shirt. She'd get in that garage sale and point stuff out to you. There's a good fork for a nickel. Yeah, that's beautiful. It's a little high. If it were three cents I'd snap it up.
—LOUIE ANDERSON

✦✦✦

My mother had morning sickness after I was born.
—RODNEY DANGERFIELD

✦✦

My mother buried three husbands, and two of them were just napping.
—RITA RUDNER

✦✦✦

I can remember the first time I had to go to sleep. Mom said, "Steven, time to go to sleep." I said, "But I don't know how." She said, "It's real easy. Just go down to the end of tired and hang a left." So I went down to the end of tired, and just out of curiosity I hung a right. My mother was there, and she said, "I thought I told you to go to sleep."
—STEVEN WRIGHT

♦♦

My mom was a ventriloquist and she always was throwing her voice. For ten years I thought the dog was telling me to kill my father.
—WENDY LIEBMAN

♦♦♦

It would seem that something which means poverty, disorder, and violence every single day should be avoided entirely. But the desire to beget children is a natural urge.
—PHYLLIS DILLER

♦♦

~✦~

A little boy watched, fascinated, as his mother covered her face in cold cream. "Why do you do that?" he asked. "To make myself beautiful." When she began to rub it off, the boy asked, "Why are you doing that? Did you give up?"

~✦~

My mom said she learned how to swim. Someone took her out in the lake and threw her off the boat. That's how she learned how to swim. I said, "Mom, they weren't trying to teach you how to swim."
—PAULA POUNDSTONE

✦✦✦

Neurotics build castles in the air; psychotics live in them. My mother cleans them.
—RITA RUDNER

✦✦

My mother never breast-fed me; she told me she only liked me as a friend.
—RODNEY DANGERFIELD

✦✦✦

My mother tried to kill me when I was a baby. She denied it. She said she thought the plastic bag would keep me fresh.
—BOB MONKHOUSE

♦♦

I asked Mom if I was a gifted child. She said they certainly wouldn't have paid for me.
—CALVIN, *CALVIN AND HOBBES*

♦♦♦

If Mama ain't happy, ain't nobody happy.
—FERRELL SIMS

♦♦

The mother-child relationship is paradoxical and, in a sense, tragic. It requires the most intense love on the mother's side, yet this very love must help the child grow away from the mother, and to become fully independent.
—ERICH FROMM

♦♦♦

A mother is not a person to lean on, but a person to make
leaning unnecessary.
—DOROTHY CANFIELD FISHER

♦♦

No woman should ever marry a man who hated his mother.
—MARTHA GELLHORN

♦♦♦

Mothers are inscrutable beings to their sons, always.
—A. E. COPPARD

♦♦

You know, Moe, my mom once said something that
really stuck with me. She said, "Homer, you're a big
disappointment," and God bless her soul,
she was really onto something.
—HOMER SIMPSON, *THE SIMPSONS*

♦♦♦

My mother's menu consisted of two choices:
Take it or leave it.
—BUDDY HACKETT

••

What my mother believed about cooking is that if you
worked hard and prospered, someone else would
do it for you.
—NORA EPHRON

•••

My mother is such a lousy cook that Thanksgiving at her
house is a time of sorrow.
—RITA RUDNER

••

My mother was a terrible cook. When I was a child I went
ice fishing. I came back with forty pounds of ice. My mother
fried it and we almost drowned.
—ANONYMOUS

•••

My mother had a great deal of trouble with me, but I think she enjoyed it.
—MARK TWAIN

◆◆

My mother loved children—she would have given anything if I had been one.
—GROUCHO MARX

◆◆◆

The phrase "working mother" is redundant.
—JANE SELLMAN

◆◆

Being a working mom is not easy. You have to be willing to screw up at every level.
—JAMI GERTZ

◆◆◆

Working mothers are guinea pigs in a scientific experiment
to show that sleep is not necessary to human life.
—ANONYMOUS

••

Republicans understand the importance of bondage between
a mother and child.
—DAN QUAYLE

•••

A mother is a person who, seeing there are only four pieces
of pie for five people, promptly announces she never did
care for pie.
—TENNEVA JORDAN

••

All women become like their mothers. That is their tragedy.
No man does. That's his.
—OSCAR WILDE

•••

The heart of a mother is a deep abyss at the bottom of which
you will always find forgiveness.
—HONORÉ DE BALZAC

••

Good moms let you lick the beaters . . . great moms
turn them off first.
—ANONYMOUS

•••

No matter how old a mother is, she watches her middle-aged
children for signs of improvement.
—FLORIDA SCOTT-MAXWELL

••

I want to have children, but my friends scare me. One told
me she was in labor for thirty-six hours. I don't even want to
do anything that feels good for thirty-six hours.
—RITA RUDNER

•••

A vacation means that the family goes away for a rest,
accompanied by mother, who sees that the others get it.
—MARCELENE COX

· ·

The joys of motherhood are never fully experienced until
the kids are in bed.
—ANONYMOUS

◆◆◆

If you have children, the demands made upon you in the first
hour of the morning can make the job of air traffic controller
seem like a walk in the park.
—ANONYMOUS

◆◆

She never quite leaves her children at home, even when she
doesn't take them along.
—MARGARET CULKIN BANNING

◆◆◆

When you are a mother, you are never really alone in your thoughts. A mother always has to think twice: once for herself, and once for her child.
—SOPHIA LOREN

••

Motherhood has a very humanizing effect. Everything gets reduced to essentials.
—MERYL STREEP

•••

A mother's happiness is like a beacon, lighting up the future but reflected also on the past in the guise of fond memories.
—HONORÉ DE BALZAC

••

With what price we pay for the glory of motherhood.
—ISADORA DUNCAN

•••

Youth fades; love droops; the leaves of friendship fall;
a mother's secret hope outlives them all.
—OLIVER WENDELL HOLMES

••

Whatever else is unsure in this stinking dunghill of a world,
a mother's love is not.
—JAMES JOYCE

•••

By and large, mothers and housewives are the only workers
who do not have regular time off. They are
the great vacation-less class.
—ANNE MORROW LINDBERGH

••

Whenever I'm with my mother, I feel as though I have to
spend the whole time avoiding land mines.
—AMY TAN

•••

There was never a child so lovely but his mother was glad to get him to sleep.
—RALPH WALDO EMERSON

••

Thanks to my mother, not a single cardboard box has found its way back into society. We receive gifts in boxes from stores that went out of business twenty years ago.
—ERMA BOMBECK

•••

Sweater, n.: garment worn by child when its mother is feeling chilly.
—AMBROSE BIERCE

••

As I have discovered by examining my past, I started out as a child. Coincidentally, so did my brother. My mother did not put all her eggs in one basket, so to speak: She gave me a younger brother named Russell, who taught me what was meant by "survival of the fittest."
—BILL COSBY

•••

Top 10 Things Mothers Are Responsible For:[5]

1. Cooking

2. Cleaning

3. Discipline

4. Homework

5. Shopping

6. Transportation

7. Playdates

8. Scheduling

9. Holidays

10. Finding Peace in the Middle East

_____

[5]   Compare with page 46.

Never lend your car to anyone to whom you have given birth.
—ERMA BOMBECK

++

Somewhere on this globe, every ten seconds, there is a
woman giving birth to a child. She must be
found and stopped.
—SAM LEVENSON

+++

Your sons weren't made to like you. That's what
grandchildren are for.
—JANE SMILEY

++

When my husband comes home, if the kids are still alive, I
figure I've done my job.
—ROSEANNE BARR

+++

I ask people why they have deer heads on their walls. They always say because it's such a beautiful animal. There you go. I think my mother is attractive, but I have photographs of her.
—ELLEN DEGENERES

~•~

A woman was walking down the street with her blouse open. A passerby stopped and said, "Excuse me Madam, but your breast is hanging out." She looked down and shrieked, "Oh my god, I left my baby on the bus!"

~•~

If there were no schools to take the children away from home part of the time, the insane asylums would be filled with mothers.
—EDWARD W. HOWE

••

Mother is far too clever to understand anything she does not like.
—ARNOLD BENNETT

•••

Every mother generally hopes that her daughter will snag a better husband than she managed to do . . . but she's certain that her boy will never get as great a wife as his father did.
—ANONYMOUS

••

My mother was like a sister to me . . . only we didn't have sex as often.
—EMO PHILIPS

•••

My mother hated me. Once, she took me to an orphanage and told me to mingle.
—PHYLLIS DILLER

••

Life is tough enough without having someone kick you from the inside.
—RITA RUDNER

•••

I found out why cats drink out of the toilet. My mother told
me it's because it's cold in there. And I'm like: How did
my mother know that?
—WENDY LIEBMAN

✦✦

My mother always told me I wouldn't amount to anything
because I procrastinate. I said, "Just wait!"
—JUDY TENUTA

✦✦✦

I've been breast-feeding for two years. I could light the
gas ring with my nipples.
—JO BRAND

✦✦

My mother wasn't the protective type. When my father left,
she told us kids, "Don't think this just had to do with me.
Your father left all of us."
—CAROLINE RHEA

✦✦✦

Don't ever tell the mother of a newborn that her baby's smile
is just gas.
—JILL WOODHULL

••

I was dating a transvestite. My mother said "Marry him,
you'll double your wardrobe!"
—JOAN RIVERS

•••

Do not join encounter groups. If you like being made to feel
inadequate, just call your mother.
—LIZ SMITH

••

A Freudian slip is when you say one thing but mean
your mother.
—ANONYMOUS

•••

There's a lot to do when you have a baby . . . like figuring out
who the father is.
—HEIDI JOYCE

' '

If you don't yell during labor, you're a fool. I screamed. Oh,
how I screamed. And that was just during the conception.
—JOAN RIVERS

+++

I was a poor kid. My mom saved money by shopping at
the Army-Navy Surplus store, but I felt stupid going to
kindergarten dressed as a Chinese General.
—ANONYMOUS

++

I have an eighteen-year-old: her name is Alexis. I chose that
name because, if I hadn't had her, I'd be driving one now.
—ROBIN FAIRBANKS

+++

I love my husband, I love my children . . . but I want
something more. Like a life.
—ROSEANNE BARR

••

The worst Mother's Day gift is sending your mother a song
over the telephone. Basically, you're putting your
mom on hold.
—CRAIG KILBORN

•••

Mother's Day is the day we honor the woman we blame for
all our personal problems.
—ANONYMOUS

••

My husband is not romantic. For Mother's Day, he gave me
a George Foreman Grill. I gave it back to him for Father's
Day, in a sort of forceful upward motion.
—SANDI SELVI

•••

My mother always said "Don't marry for money . . . divorce
for money."
—WENDY LIEBMAN

✦✦

I've been married fourteen years and I have three kids.
Obviously, I breed well in captivity.
—ROSEANNE BARR

✦✦✦

I'd like to have kids. I get those maternal feelings. Like when
I'm lying on the couch and can't reach the remote.
—KATHLEEN MADIGAN

✦✦

My mother has gossip dyslexia. She has to talk in front of
other people's backs.
—RICHARD LEWIS

✦✦✦

I asked my mother if I was adopted. She said, "Not yet,
but we placed an ad."
—DANA SNOW

++

My mother from time to time puts on her wedding dress.
Not that she's sentimental . . . she just gets a little behind
in her laundry.
—BRIAN KILEY

+++

My mom will wake me up at six in the morning and say,
"The early bird catches the worm." Mom, if I want a worm,
I'll drink a bottle of tequila."
—PAM STONE

++

When we were growing up, my mother told my brother
he was a pain in the neck; he became a chiropractor.
Thankfully, she didn't say he was a pain in the ass.
—JOEL WARSHAW

✦✦✦

You can put up a front in the real world, but your mom sees
through that faster than Superman sees through
Lois Lane's pantsuit.
—DENNIS MILLER

✦✦

Hey, Mother, I come bearing a gift. I'll give you a hint: It's in
my diaper and it's not a toaster.
—STEWIE GRIFFIN, *FAMILY GUY*

✦✦✦

I'm not a breeder. I have no maternal instincts whatsoever.
I ovulate sand.
—MARGARET CHO

◆◆

As long as a woman can look ten years younger than her
own daughter, she is perfectly satisfied.
—OSCAR WILDE

◆◆◆

Few misfortunes can befall a boy which bring worse consequences than to have a really affectionate mother.

—SOMERSET MAUGHAM

◆◆

I want my children to have all the things I couldn't afford.
Then I want to move in with them.
—PHYLLIS DILLER

◆◆◆

Match the Quote to the Movie: Mother Edition[6]

A. *Mamma Mia!*   D. *Wyatt Earp*
B. *Mask*   E. *Psycho*
C. *Step Brothers*

~+~

1. My Mama always said don't put off 'til tomorrow who you can kill today.
2. Somebody up there has got it in for me. I bet it's my mother.
3. I swear, I'm so pissed off at my mom. As soon as she's of age, I'm putting her in a home.
4. A boy's best friend is his mother.
5. First you told me he was gonna be retarded, then you told me he was gonna be blind AND deaf. If I'd dug his grave every time one of you geniuses told me he was gonna die, I'd be eating chop suey in China by now!

---

[6]   1. D., 2. A., 3. C., 4. E., 5. B.

Fatherhood

Never raise your hands to your kids. It leaves
your groin unprotected.

—RED BUTTONS

DADS HAVE ALWAYS GOTTEN a bum rap.
"Wait until your father gets home!"

"When your father hears about this, there will be hell
to pay!"

"Go ask your father and don't bother me."

Disciplinarian, boogeyman, bad cop . . . you name it and
that was the role good ole dad was often asked to fill at one
time or another . . . and was usually good at.

Still, they get the short end of the stick every time . . .

The crappy tie at Xmas and the ugly sweater on Father's
Day. Most typically forgotten in the Oscar speech. Pretty
much never included in the dedication of the horrific tell-all
the kids eventually write about them.

More than enough to make and keep one snarky? You
betcha.

Here are some of the snarkier instances where dads bit back.

I have good kids. I'm trying to bring them up the right way,
not spanking them. I find waving the gun around
gets the same job done.
—DENIS LEARY

••

You wake up one day and say, "I don't think I ever need to
sleep or have sex again." Congratulations, you're ready
to have children.
—RAY ROMANO

•••

There are no perfect parents. Even Jesus had a distant father
and a domineering mother. I'd have trust issues if my father
allowed me to be crucified.
—BOB SMITH

••

If the new American father feels bewildered and even
defeated, let him take comfort from the fact that whatever
he does in any fathering situation has a fifty percent chance
of being right.
—BILL COSBY

•••

I've got seven kids. The three words you hear most around my house are: hello, goodbye, and I'm pregnant.
—DEAN MARTIN

••

No man is responsible for his father. That was entirely his mother's affair.
—MARGARET TURNBULL

•••

To be a successful father there's one absolute rule: When you have a kid, don't look at it for the first two years.
—ERNEST HEMINGWAY

••

I want my kids to have the things in life that I never had when I was growing up. Things like beards and chest hair.
—JAROD KINTZ

•••

Fatherhood is pretending the present you love most
is soap-on-a-rope.
—BILL COSBY

••

That is the thankless position of the father in the family:
The provider for all and the enemy of all.
—J. AUGUST STRINDBERG

•••

By the time a man realizes that maybe his father was right,
he usually has a son who thinks he's wrong.
—CHARLES WADSWORTH

••

When I was a boy of fourteen, my father was so ignorant I
could hardly stand to have the old man around. But when I
got to be twenty-one, I was astonished at how much the old
man had learned in seven years.
—MARK TWAIN

•••

The thing to remember about fathers is . . . they're men. A
girl has to keep it in mind: They are dragon-seekers, bent on
improbable rescues. Scratch any father, you find someone
chock-full of qualms and romantic terrors, believing change
is a threat, like your first shoes with heels on, like your first
bicycle . . .
—PHYLLIS McGINLEY

~+~

*Dad had once said, Trust your mind, Rob. If
it smells like shit but has writing across it that
says Happy Birthday and a candle stuck down
in it, what is it?*
Is there icing on it? he'd said.
*Dad had done that thing of squinting his eyes
when an answer was not quite there yet.*
—*GEORGE SAUNDERS*

~+~

More of the Worst Parenting Books of All Time

Siblings Without Rivalry: Keeping Separate Households in Different States
The Happiest Toddler on the Block: The Joys of Ritalin
The No-Cry Sleep Solution by Jack Daniels
The Baby Bond: 50 Shades of Spit-Up

Sir Walter, being strangely surprised and put out of his countenance at so great a table, gives his son a damned blow over the face. His son, as rude as he was, would not strike his father, but strikes over the face the gentleman that sat next to him and said, "Box about: Twill come to my father anon."

—JOHN AUBREY

++

I didn't make Dale Jr. go be a racer. The kid wanted to be a racer. I'd just as soon him be a doctor, a preacher, or whatever. I'm not sure I'd want him to be a lawyer.

—DALE EARNHARDT

+++

Before I was married, I had a hundred theories about raising
children and no children. Now, I have three children
and no theories.
—JOHN WILMOT

••

A father is a man who carries pictures where his money
used to be.
—ANONYMOUS

•••

The place of the father in the modern suburban family is a
very small one, particularly if he plays golf.
—BERTRAND RUSSELL

••

A father is always making his baby into a little woman.
And when she is a woman, he turns her back again.
—ENID BAGNOLD

•••

My father never raised his hand to any one of his children,
except in self-defense.
—FRED ALLEN

◆◆

When I was a kid, I used to imagine animals running under
my bed. I told my dad, and he solved the problem quickly.
He cut the legs off the bed.
—LOU BROCK

◆◆◆

My father carries around the picture of the kid that
came with the wallet.
—RODNEY DANGERFIELD

◆◆

Undeservedly you will atone for the sins of your fathers.
—HORACE

◆◆◆

I grew up to have my father's looks, my father's speech patterns, my father's posture, my father's walk, my father's opinions, and my mother's contempt for my father.
—JULES FEIFFER

••

My father hated radio and he could not wait for television to be invented so that he could hate that, too.
—PETER DE VRIES

•••

My father confused me. From the ages of one to seven, I thought my name was Jesus Christ!
—BILL COSBY

••

My father only hit me once—but he used a Volvo.
—BOB MONKHOUSE

•••

Dad always thought laughter was the best medicine, which I guess is why several of us died of tuberculosis.

—JACK HANDY

••

I never got along with my dad. Kids used to come up to me and say, "My dad can beat up your dad." I'd say, "Yeah? When?"

—BILL HICKS

•••

It's not easy to juggle a pregnant wife and a troubled child, but somehow I managed to fit in eight hours of TV a day.

—HOMER SIMPSON, *THE SIMPSONS*

••

I remember the time I was kidnapped and they sent a piece of my finger to my father. He said he wanted more proof.

—RODNEY DANGERFIELD

•••

I've got two wonderful children—two out of five isn't bad, right?
—HENNY YOUNGMAN

••

Perhaps host and guest is really the happiest relation for a father and son.
—EVELYN WAUGH

•••

I have seen more men destroyed by the desire to have a wife and child and to keep them in comfort that I have seen destroyed by drinks and harlots.
—WILLIAM BUTLER YEATS

••

Fathers should never be seen nor heard. That is the only proper basis for family life.
—OSCAR WILDE

•••

Top 10 Things Fathers Are Responsible For:

1. Sports

2. Teaching them how to defend themselves

3. Movies

4. Beer (to relax from all the work it took for 1–3)

5. See Mom's list

6. See Mom's list

7. See Mom's list

8. See Mom's list

9. See Mom's list

10. See Mom's list

I can't get past the fact that food is now coming out of my wife's breasts. What was once essentially an entertainment center is now a juice bar.
—PAUL KRUGMAN

◆◆

My father would say things that made no sense, like, "If I were the last person on earth, some moron would turn left in front of me!"
—LOUIE ANDERSON

◆◆◆

My wife just let me know I'm about to become a father for the first time. The bad news is we already have two kids.
—BRIAN KILEY

◆◆

My father was cheap. He'd make us Hamburger Helper with no hamburger.
—A. J. JAMAL

◆◆◆

My dad said he had a tough childhood. He had to walk twenty miles to school in five feet of snow . . . and he was only four feet tall.

—DANA EAGLE

++

When you're young, you think your dad is Superman. When you grow up, you realize he's just a guy who wears a cape.

—DAVE ATTELL

+++

My father didn't ask me to leave home. He took me down to the highway and pointed.

—HENNY YOUNGMAN

++

My dad's pants kept creeping up on him. By the time he was sixty-five, he was just a pair of pants and a head.

—JEFF ALTMAN

+++

I have mixed emotions when I receive my Father's Day gifts.
I'm glad my children remember me; I'm disappointed that
they actually think I dress that way.
—MIKE DUGAN

++

Father's Day: For that lethal combination of alcohol and
new power tools.
—DAVID LETTERMAN

+++

I was raised just by my mother. My father died when I was
eight years old . . . at least, that's what he told us
in the letter.
—DREW CAREY

++

I'm getting ready to be a parent. I just turned thirty and
I'm getting tired of mowing my grass.
—JEFF FOXWORTHY

+++

Sorry, Meg. Daddy loves ya, but Daddy also loves *Star Trek*,
and in all fairness, *Star Trek* was here first.
—PETER GRIFFIN, *FAMILY GUY*

••

A father is a banker provided by nature.
—FRENCH PROVERB

•••

My father was frightened of his father, I was frightened of
my father, and I am damned well going to see to it that
my children are frightened of me.
—KING GEORGE V

••

The child had every toy his father wanted.
—ROBERT C. WHITTEN

•••

When I was born my father spent three weeks trying to find
a loophole in my birth certificate.
—JACKIE VERNON

••

He became a father today. There'll be hell to pay
if his wife finds out.
—ANONYMOUS

++

Today, while the titular head of the family may still be the
father, everyone knows that he is little more than chairman,
at most, of the entertainment committee.
—ASHLEY MONTAGU

+++

The fundamental defect of fathers is that they want their
children to be a credit to them.
—BERTRAND RUSSELL

++

It is a wise child that knows its own father, and an
unusual one that unreservedly approves of him.
—MARK TWAIN

+++

Watching your daughter being collected by her date feels like handing over a million dollar Stradivarius to a gorilla.
—JIM BISHOP

♦♦♦

I have adapted the philosophy of Genghis Khan, "Give a man a fish and he eats for a day, teach a man to fish and he eats forever." My slogan is, "Show a teenage boy a gun, and he'll have your daughter home by 11:30."
—SINBAD

♦♦

I married your mother because I wanted children. Imagine my disappointment when you arrived.
—GROUCHO MARX

♦♦♦

A father is a man who expects his son to be as good a man as he meant to be.

—FRANK A. CLARK

♦♦

Match the Quote to the Movie: Father Edition[7]

A. *Fight Club*
B. *Father of the Bride*
C. *Empire Falls*

D. *3 Men and a Baby*
E. *A Chorus Line*

1. -Drive carefully. And don't forget to fasten your condom.
   -Dad!
   -Seat belt! I meant, I meant seat belt.
2. I couldn't catch a ball if it had Elmer's Glue all over it. And my father had to be this ex-football star. He didn't know what to tell his friends, so he told them all I had polio. On Father's Day, I used to limp for him.
3. All we have to do is feed it, it'll shut up.
4. Shut up! Our fathers were our models for God. If our fathers bailed, what does that tell you about God?
5. To tell you the truth, I would rather have a complete idiot for a child than an ingrate.

---

[7]   1. B., 2. E., 3. D., 4. A., 5. C.

Children

We had a C-section. That's when the baby comes out
like toast.

—BOBCAT GOLDTHWAIT

KIDS . . . WHAT'S THE MATTER with kids
today . . .

That's the beginning lyric from one of the more memorable songs from the 1963 musical *Bye Bye Birdie* . . .

First, let me go on record as saying that, for the most part, I love kids. Repeat: Love 'em.

They're usually good for a ton of laughs, say the darndest things . . . and generally are cute and adorable and all that good stuff.

And when friends with kids come to the house, I pretty much always love it when they come . . . and love it when they go. Small doses. I'll partake in the fun stuff, you handle the cranky.

I'm not alone here. It's a view widely held by a growing lot of people, many of whom are both with kids and without kids.

Those without usually say the same thing—they affect your career, your marriage, your bank account, your piece of mind, your social life, and, most definitely, your sleep patterns. It's become a movement, with "non-parent" groups popping up all over the place.

Of those with kids, when pushed into a corner, they will reluctantly admit that, if they had it to do over again, they would maybe/possibly/probably do it differently . . . maybe two instead of six . . . maybe wait more than ten months in between 1 & 2 & 3. . . . And some even say they might have even waited a few years after marriage until the first one. Always accompanied by a wistful look in their eye. . . . Which they quickly shake off and aver how much they love their kids.

Not in question. But we all agree they can be a handful and can easily get on your last nerve . . . proven by these snarky quotes from almost every generation. Take a look.

Familiarity breeds contempt—and children.
—MARK TWAIN

••

The quickest way for a parent to get a child's attention is to sit down and look comfortable.
—LANE OLINHOUSE

•••

A three-year-old child is a being who gets almost as much fun out of a fifty-six-dollar set of swings as it does out of finding a small green worm.
—BILL VAUGHAN

✦✦

In the little world in which children have their existence, whosoever brings them up, there is nothing so finely perceived and so finely felt as injustice.
—CHARLES DICKENS

✦✦✦

It is amazing how quickly the kids learn to drive a car, yet are unable to understand the lawnmower, snow blower, or vacuum cleaner.
—BEN BERGOR

✦✦

Like all parents, my husband and I just do the best we can, and hold our breath, and hope we've set aside enough money to pay for our kids' therapy.
—MICHELLE PFEIFFER

✦✦✦

The truth is that parents are not really interested in justice.
They just want quiet.
—BILL COSBY

++

Raising kids is part joy and part guerrilla warfare.
—ED ASNER

+++

Parents are the bones on which children cut their teeth.
—PETER USTINOV

++

If you want children to keep their feet on the ground,
put some responsibility on their shoulders.
—ABIGAIL VAN BUREN

+++

Don't handicap your children by making their lives easy.
—ROBERT A. HEINLEIN

••

Although there are many trial marriages . . . there is
no such thing as a trial child.
—GAIL SHEEHY

•••

Each day of our lives we make deposits in the memory banks
of our children.
—CHARLES R. SWINDOLL

••

If nature had arranged that husbands and wives should have
children alternatively, there would never be more than
three in a family.
—LAWRENCE HOUSMAN

•••

Even when freshly washed and relieved of all obvious confections, children tend to be sticky.

—FRAN LEBOWITZ

++

If you have never been hated by your child you have never been a parent.

—BETTE DAVIS

+++

Even very young children need to be informed about dying. Explain the concept of death very carefully to your child. This will make threatening him with it much more effective.

—P. J. O'ROURKE

++

You can learn many things from children . . . how much patience you have, for instance.

—FRANKLIN P. JONES

+++

Children are natural mimics who act like their parents, despite every effort to teach them good manners.
—ANONYMOUS

••

The most important thing that parents can teach their children is how to get along without them.
—FRANK A. CLARK

•••

People who say they sleep like a baby usually don't have one.
—LEO BURKE

••

You know your children are growing up when they stop asking you where they came from and refuse to tell you where they're going.
—P. J. O'ROURKE

•••

I was cesarean born. You can't really tell, although whenever
I leave a house now, I go out through a window.
—STEVEN WRIGHT

••

When a child is allowed to do absolutely as he pleases, it will
not be long until nothing pleases him.
—ANONYMOUS

•••

Everyone is in awe of the lion tamer in a cage with half a
dozen lions—everyone but a school bus driver.
—ANONYMOUS

••

Families with babies and families without are
so sorry for each other.
—EDWARD W. HOWE

•••

Parenthood: That state of being better chaperoned than you were before marriage.
—MARCELENE COX

♦♦

Life was a lot simpler when what we honored was Father and Mother rather than all major credit cards.
—ROBERT ORBEN

♦♦♦

The way I wrestle five-year-olds makes me think if I were ever attacked by a pack of midgets, I'd be okay.
—JAROD KINTZ

♦♦

Children begin by loving their parents; after a time they judge them; rarely, if ever, do they forgive them.
—OSCAR WILDE

♦♦♦

Everyone should have kids. They are the greatest joy in the world. But they are also terrorists. You'll realize this as soon as they are born, and they start using sleep deprivation to break you.

—RAY ROMANO

••

Children really brighten up a household—they never turn the lights off.

—RALPH BUS

•••

Kids. They're not easy. But there has to be some penalty for sex.

—BILL MAHER

••

You don't have favorites among your children, but you do have allies.

—ZADIE SMITH

•••

There is only one pretty child in the world, and every mother
has it.
—CHINESE PROVERB

♦♦

Mom and Dad say I should make my life an example of the
principles I believe in. But every time I do, they tell me
to stop it.
—CALVIN, *CALVIN AND HOBBES*

♦♦♦

Grown-ups never understand anything by themselves, and it
is tiresome for children to be always and forever explaining
things to them.
—ANTOINE DE SAINT-EXUPÉRY

♦♦

Children aren't coloring books. You don't get to fill them
with your favorite colors.
—KHALED HOSSEINI

♦♦♦

Schizoid behavior is a pretty common thing in children.
It's accepted, because all we adults have this unspoken
agreement that children are lunatics.
—STEPHEN KING

••

The best way to keep children at home is to make the home
atmosphere pleasant . . . and let the air out of the tires.
—DOROTHY PARKER

•••

If your parents never had children, chances are
you won't either.
—DICK CAVETT

••

Always be nice to your children because they are the ones
who will choose your rest home.
—PHYLLIS DILLER

•••

Top 10 Lies Children Tell Their Parents:

1. I didn't do it.

2. I didn't do it.

3. I didn't do it.

4. I didn't do it.

5. He/She did it.

6. I didn't do it.

7. I didn't do it.

8. I didn't do it.

9. I didn't do it.

10. I really didn't do it.

My childhood should have taught me lessons for my own
parenthood, but it didn't, because parenting can be learned
only by people who have no children.

—BILL COSBY

++

Parents like the idea of kids, they just don't like their kids.

—MORLEY SAFER

+++

Smack your child every day. If you don't know
why—he does.

—JOEY ADAMS

++

Don't try to make children grow up to be like you,
or they may do it.

—RUSSELL BAKER

+++

Children are a great comfort in your old age—and they help
you reach it faster, too.
—LIONEL KAUFFMAN

✦✦

I take my children everywhere, but they always find their
way back home.
—ROBERT ORBEN

✦✦✦

Youth is a wonderful thing. What a crime to waste it
on children.
—GEORGE BERNARD SHAW

✦✦

Providence protects children and idiots. I know because
I have tested it.
—MARK TWAIN

✦✦✦

I've noticed that one thing about parents is that no matter what stage your child is in, the parents who have older children always tell you the next stage is worse.
—DAVE BARRY

◆◆

One thing they never tell you about child raising is that for the rest of your life, at the drop of a hat, you are expected to know your child's name and how old he or she is.
—ERMA BOMBECK

◆◆◆

The trouble with children is that they are not returnable.
—QUENTIN CRISP

◆◆

My husband and I are either going to buy a dog or have a child. We can't decide whether to ruin our carpet or ruin our lives.
—RITA RUDNER

◆◆◆

Human beings are the only creatures that allow
their children to come back home.
—BILL COSBY

✦✦

Parents are the last people on earth who ought to have
children.
—SAMUEL BUTLER

✦✦✦

I want to have children and I know my time is running out:
I want to have them while my parents are still young enough
to take care of them.
—RITA RUDNER

✦✦

Madam, there's no such thing as a tough child—if you
parboil them first for seven hours, they always
come out tender.
—W. C. FIELDS

✦✦✦

Pretty much all the honest truth telling there is in the world
is done by children.
—OLIVER WENDELL HOLMES

••

In automobile terms, the child supplies the power but the
parents have to do the steering.
—DR. BENJAMIN SPOCK

•••

Experts say you should never hit your children in anger.
When is a good time? When you're feeling festive?
—ROSEANNE BARR

••

Kids are wonderful . . . I like mine barbecued.
—BOB HOPE

•••

Ask your child what he wants for dinner only if he's buying.
—FRAN LEBOWITZ

◆◆◆

I wish to thank my parents for making it all possible . . . and
I wish to thank my children for making it necessary.
—VICTOR BORGE

◆◆

Most children threaten at times to run away from home.
This is the only thing that keeps some parents going.
—PHYLLIS DILLER

◆◆◆

Telling a teenager the facts of life is like giving a fish a bath.
—ARNOLD H. GLASOW

••

One cannot love lumps of flesh, and little infants are
nothing more.
—SAMUEL JOHNSON

•••

If thine enemy offends thee, give his child a drum.
—FRAN LEBOWITZ

••

Even as kids reach adolescence, they need more than ever for
us to watch over them. Adolescence is not about letting go.
It's about hanging on during a very bumpy ride.
—RON TAFFEL

•••

Of children as of procreation—the pleasure momentary,
the posture ridiculous, the expense, damnable.
—EVELYN WAUGH

✦✦

Few things are more satisfying than seeing your children
have teenagers of their own.
—DOUG LARSON

✦✦✦

Childhood, *n*.: The period of human life intermediate
between the idiocy of infancy and the folly of youth—two
removes from the sin of manhood and from the
remorse of age.
—AMBROSE BIERCE

✦✦

Nobody gets out of childhood alive.
—HARLAN ELLISON

✦✦✦

Children should neither be seen nor heard from—ever again.
—W. C. FIELDS

••

There are three terrible ages of childhood: 1 to 10, 10 to 20, and 20 to 30.
—CLEVELAND AMORY

•••

Parents were invented to make children happy by giving them something to ignore.
—OGDEN NASH

••

They grow up so slow.
—BRUCE ERIC KAPLAN

✦✦✦

Children are the most desirable opponents at scrabble as they are both easy to beat and fun to cheat.
—FRAN LEBOWITZ

~✦~

A man calls the hospital in a state of panic. "My wife is pregnant and the contractions are only two minutes apart!" The doctor asks, "Is this her first child?" The man responds, "No, you idiot, this is her husband!"

~✦~

To an adolescent, there is nothing in the world more embarrassing than a parent.
—DAVE BARRY

✦✦

Once you have children, it forever changes the way you
bore other people.
—BRUCE ERIC KAPLAN

✦✦✦

As a teenager you are at the last stage in your life when you
will be happy to hear that the phone is for you.

—FRAN LEBOWITZ

✦✦

Heredity is what sets the parents of a teenager wondering
about each other.
—LAURENCE J. PETER

✦✦✦

Adolescence is just one big walking pimple.
—CAROL BURNETT

✦✦

Adorable children are considered to be the general property of the entire human race. Rude children belong to their mothers.

—JUDITH MARTIN

✦✦✦

I had a Jewish delivery. They knock you out with the first pain and wake you up when the hairdresser gets there.

—JOAN RIVERS

~✦~

At the age of four, George S. Kaufman was told his aunt was coming to visit and asked, "It wouldn't hurt to be nice to her; would it?" to which he replied, "That depends on your threshold of pain."

~✦~

You can't scare me. I have children!

—GARFIELD

✦✦

Having children makes you no more a parent than having a
piano makes you a pianist.
—MICHAEL LEVINE

◆◆◆

A baby is a loud noise at one end and no sense of
responsibility at the other.
—RONALD KNOX

◆◆

The first half of our life is ruined by our parents, and the
second half by our children.

—CLARENCE DARROW

◆◆◆

I could tell my parents hated me. My bath toys were
a toaster and a radio.
—RODNEY DANGERFIELD

◆◆

It's no wonder that people are so horrible—they start life
as children.
—KINGSLEY AMIS

✦✦✦

My parents used to take me to Lewis's Department Store in
Glasgow. They were skinflints, they used to take me to the
pet department and tell me it was the zoo.
—BILLY CONNOLLY

✦✦

A parent who has never apologized to his children is a
monster. If he's always apologizing, his children
are monsters.

—MIGNON MCLAUGHLIN

✦✦✦

I don't think my parents liked me. They put a live teddy bear
in my crib.
—WOODY ALLEN

✦✦

Oh, to be only half as wonderful as my child thought I was
when he was small, and only half as stupid as my teenager
now thinks I am.
—REBECCA RICHARDS

✦✦✦

There's nothing wrong with teenagers that reasoning with
them won't aggravate.
—JEAN KERR

✦✦

To lose one parent may be regarded as a misfortune; to lose
both looks like carelessness.

—OSCAR WILDE

✦✦✦

When I was kidnapped, my parents snapped into action.
They rented out my room.
—WOODY ALLEN

✦✦

I was going through puberty at the same time my mother was going through the change. The menfolk stayed away.
—JULIE WALTERS

***

There is no one thirstier than a four-year-old that has just gone to bed.
—FRAN LEBOWITZ

**

I have found the best way to give advice to your children is to find out what they want and then advise them to do it.

—HARRY S. TRUMAN

***

Oh, why will parents always appear at the wrong time? Some extraordinary mistake in nature, I suppose.
—OSCAR WILDE

**

A child is a curly, dimpled lunatic.
—RALPH WALDO EMERSON

✦✦✦

Always end the name of your child with a vowel, so that
when you yell, the name will carry.

—BILL COSBY

✦✦✦

Everybody knows how to raise children, except the people
who have them.
—P. J. O'ROURKE

✦✦

My parents brought me up with three magic words—total sensory deprivation.
—EMO PHILIPS

✦✦✦

Do not, on a rainy day, ask your child what he feels like doing, because I assure you that what he feels like doing, you won't feel like watching.
—FRAN LEBOWITZ

✦✦

There are times when parenthood seems like nothing more than feeding the hand that bites you.

—PETER DE VRIES

✦✦✦

A two-year-old is like having a blender, but you don't have a top for it.
—JERRY SEINFELD

✦✦

One of the first things you notice about a backward country
is the way the children obey their parents.
—ERMA BOMBECK

•••

Alligators have the right idea—they eat their young.
—EVE ARDEN, IN *MILDRED PIERCE*

••

We spend the first twelve months teaching them to walk and
talk, and the next twelve years telling them to sit down
and shut up.

—PHYLLIS DILLER

•••

Children are unpredictable. You never know what
inconsistency they're going to catch you in next.
—FRANKLIN P. JONES

••

The real menace in dealing with a five-year-old is that in no time at all you begin to sound like a five-year-old.
—JEAN KERR

✦✦✦

I'm getting to the age where I'm thinking about having step-kids of my own . . . maybe a thirteen-year-old daughter to bond with. Take her out, get her tattooed or something. I don't care, she's not my kid.
—TRACEY SMITH

✦✦

If you must hold yourself up to your children as an object lesson, hold yourself up as a warning and not as an example.

—GEORGE BERNARD SHAW

✦✦✦

I don't visit my parents because Delta Airlines won't wait in the yard while I run in.
—MARGARET SMITH

✦✦

I adopted a baby. I originally wanted a highway, but there
was a lot of red tape.
—MARGARET SMITH

✦✦✦

My childhood was kind of a blur. To tell you the truth,
I probably needed better glasses.
—WENDY LIEBMAN

~✦~

*I asked my friend who has children, "What if I
have a baby, dedicate my life to it, and it grows
up to hate me?" She said, "What do you mean,
'if?'"*

~✦~

You have to change those diapers every day. It says "six to
twelve pounds" on the side on the box. They're not lying,
that's all those things hold.
—JEFF FOXWORTHY

✦✦

A child is too old to breast-feed when he can unhook
mommy's bra with one hand.
—ANTHONY CLARK

♦♦♦

I hate changing my son's diapers after he comes home from
daycare. I know exactly what he ate. Yesterday it was carrots.
Tomorrow I'm hoping for long-stemmed roses.
—SHIRLEY LIPNER

♦♦

In the beginning, you always get drugs when you take the
baby to see the doctor. The drugs are for the parents.

—ANONYMOUS

♦♦♦

Studies show rectal thermometers are still the best way to
take a baby's temperature . . . plus, it really shows them
who's boss.
—TINA FEY

♦♦

~♦~

*I asked my husband if he wanted to be in the
same room with me when I gave birth. He said,
"It would have to be a big room, and there
would have to be a bar at one end."*

~♦~

When I was a baby, I kept a diary. I was rereading it recently.
It said: "Day One: Still tired from the move.
Day Two: Everybody talks to me like I'm an idiot."
—STEVEN WRIGHT

♦♦

My friends always want to show me films of the baby's birth.
No thanks . . . but I'll look at video of the conception,
if you've got one.
—GARRY SHANDLING

♦♦♦

Children are smarter than any of us. Know how I know
that? I don't know one child with a full-time job
and children.

—BILL HICKS

✦✦✦

Since childhood is a time when kids prepare to be grown-
ups, I think it makes a lot of sense to traumatize your
children. Gets 'em ready for the real world.

—GEORGE CARLIN

✦✦

Children are contemptuous, haughty, irritable, envious,
sneaky, selfish, lazy, flighty, timid, liars and hypocrites,
quick to laugh and cry, extreme in expressing joy and sorrow,
especially about trifles, they'll do anything to avoid pain but
they enjoy inflicting it: Little men already.

—JEAN DE LA BRUYÈRE

✦✦✦

In general, my kids refused to eat anything that hadn't
danced on TV.

—ERMA BOMBECK

✦✦

Children ask better questions than adults. "May I have a cookie?" "Why is the sky blue?" and "What does a cow say?" are far more likely to elicit a cheerful response than "Where's your manuscript?" "Why haven't you called?" and "Who's your lawyer?"

—FRAN LEBOWITZ

♦♦

In America there are two classes of travel: first class, and with children.

—ROBERT BENCHLEY

♦♦♦

Any kid will run any errand for you if you ask at bedtime.

—RED SKELTON

♦♦

Children seldom misquote. In fact, they usually repeat word for word what you shouldn't have said.

—ANONYMOUS

♦♦♦

What is a home without children? Quiet.
—HENNY YOUNGMAN

◆◆

There is a pervasive tendency to treat children as adults,
and adults as children. The options of children are thus
steadily expanded, while those of adults are progressively
constricted. The result is unruly children and
childish adults.
—THOMAS SZASZ

◆◆◆

Labor Day is a glorious holiday because your child will be
going back to school the next day. It would have been called
Independence Day, but that name was already taken.
—BILL DODDS

◆◆

Before I got married, I had six theories about bringing up
children; now I have six children, and no theories.
—JOHN WILMOT

◆◆◆

What's the best way to keep a two-year-old from biting their fingernails? Make them change their own diapers.
—PAUL LYNDE

+++

I lived at home until my mid-twenties, with my mother. If you're twenty-five and still sleeping on *Star Wars* sheets, the force is not with you.
—GARY GULMAN

++

Fortunately, my parents were intelligent, enlightened people. The accepted me for what I was: a punishment from God.
—DAVID STEINBERG

+++

Match the Quote to the Movie: Children Edition[8]

A. *Hot Fuzz*
B. *Finding Neverland*
C. *Spy Kids*

D. *Up*
E. *Beauty and the Beast*

~•~

1. -Do you want to play a game? It's called "See Who Can Go the Longest Without Saying Anything."
   -Cool! My mom loves that game!
2. - It's Frank! He's appointed himself Judge, Jury, and Executioner.
   - He is not Judge Judy and Executioner!
3. Do I still have to sleep in the cupboard?
4. Our parents can't be spies . . . they're not cool enough!
5. - This is Jack. Second in line to the throne. And that one's Michael. He's only five.
   - And I'm in prison for it.

[8]   1. D., 2. A., 3. E., 4. C., 5. B.

Siblings

Having one child makes you a parent; having two
makes you a referee.
—DAVID FROST

YOU CAN EASILY MAKE the argument that no one
can piss you off, anger you, frustrate you . . . or cause as
much consternation as your siblings. You know why? They're you.

Slightly different in appearance, occasionally opposite in
temperament, possibly saner.

And they know stuff. They know about past indiscretions, foibles, weaknesses, secrets, faults, history of mortifications, and, above all, breaking points. No one can push a
button or cut to the quick with a snark like a brother or a sister.

Not that it's all bad. Siblings also share inside jokes,
family history, forgotten covert plots against the head(s) of
the family,[9] buried treasures, and first occurrences.

They can be your strongest defender against the world . . .
AFTER they've knocked you around a bit.

Herein are some choice snarks about the relationship
most often called a double-edged sword.

---

[9] See *The Godfather, Part II*

More than Santa Claus, your sister knows when you've been bad and good.
—LINDA SUNSHINE

••

Big sisters are the crab grass in the lawn of life.
—CHARLES M. SCHULZ

••

When I was a kid, we had a quicksand box in the backyard. I was an only child . . . eventually.
—STEVEN WRIGHT

•••

If you don't understand how a woman could both love her sister dearly and want to wring her neck at the same time, then you were probably an only child.
—LINDA SUNSHINE

••

If you want to know how your girl will treat you after
marriage, just listen to her talking to her little brother.
—SAM LEVENSON

••

Top 5 Dumbest Toys Ever

Clackers: Two heavy, solid balls on a string with a stick to
swing them at top speeds . . . as used on *Game of Thrones*?

Jarts: For that perfect puncture wound.

A "real" Easy Bake Oven: Nothin' says lovin' like third-degree
burns from the oven!

The Pez Gun: "Let me get this straight . . . you invented a toy
that shoots tiny bits of candy down a child's throat at
high speeds? Cool! Who do I make the check out to?"

Creepy Crawler ThingMaker: More melted plastic placed in
molds and cooked at extremely high temps. . . . Nothin'
makes something creepier than real skin singed onto the
mold!

My sister's asthmatic. In the middle of an asthma attack she got an obscene phone call. The guy said, "Did I call you or did you call me?"
—JOHN MENDOZA

✦✦✦

The best way to get a puppy is to beg for a baby brother— and they'll settle for a puppy every time.
—WINSTON PENDELTON

✦✦

I grew up with six brothers. It's how I learned to dance— waiting for the bathroom.
—BOB HOPE

✦✦✦

I had older brothers. Growing up the only girl in a family is like growing up to be a tropical fruit drink . . . somewhere between being spoiled rotten and beaten to a pulp.
—DIANE FORD

✦✦

I was the youngest of five boys. After they had me, Mom and
Dad never spoke to each other again.
—BOB HOPE

◆◆◆

My brother is gay but my parents don't care . . . as long as he
marries a doctor.
—ELAYNE BOOSLER

◆◆

Never praise a sister to a sister in the hope of your
compliments reaching the proper ears.
—RUDYARD KIPLING

◆◆◆

Never let an angry sister comb your hair.
—PATRICIA McCANN

◆◆

Top 10 Lies Parents Tell Their Children:

1. Eat your vegetables and you'll grow up big and strong.

2. If you're not good, I'm calling Santa.

3. It's a grown-up haircut.

4. It tastes like chicken.

5. All the kids are wearing them.

6. Your teacher called and said you have to spend more time on your homework.

7. After a while, nobody will even notice your braces.

8. It's not about winning, it's about going out and having fun.

9. Someday you'll thank me.

10. You're not fat.

I am an only child. I have one sister.
—WOODY ALLEN

◆◆

If your sister is in a hurry to go out and won't catch your eye,
she's wearing your best sweater.
—PAM BROWN

◆◆◆

Comparison is a death knell to sibling harmony.
—ELIZABETH FISHES

◆◆

Each generation has been an education for us in different
ways. The first child-with-bloody-nose was rushed to the
emergency room. The fifth child-with-bloody-nose was told
to go to the yard immediately and stop bleeding
on the carpet.
—ART LINKLETTER

◆◆◆

I practice birth control, which is being around my sister's children. You want to run right out and ovulate after you play with them for five minutes.
—BRETT BUTLER

++

My sister wanted to be an actress. She never made it, but she does live in a trailer . . . so she got halfway. She's an actress; she's just never called to the set.
—MITCH HEDBERG

+++

There is a little boy inside the man who is my brother. . . . Oh, how I hated that little boy. And how I love him, too.
—ANNA QUINDLEN

++

My brother is gay; he went to London only to find out that Big Ben was a clock.
—RODNEY DANGERFIELD

+++

Match the Quote to the Movie: Siblings Edition[10]

A. *Harry Potter and the Sorcerer's Stone* D. *The Godfather, Part II*
B. *The Godfather, Part I*   E. *The Parent Trap*
C. *Home for the Holidays*   F. *Chinatown*

~ + ~

1. I know it was you. You broke my heart. You broke my heart!

2. Come on, you think I'd make my sister a widow?

3. - She's my daughter [slap]
   - I said I want the truth!
   - She's my sister . . . [slap] She's my daughter . . .
   - [Slap] My sister, my daughter . . .
   - [More slaps] She's my sister AND my daughter!

4. - You don't know the first thing about me.
   - Likewise, I'm sure. If I just met you on the street . . .
     if you gave me your phone number . . . I'd throw it away.
   - Well, we don't have to like each other, Jo. We're family.

5. - Fred, you next.
   - He's not Fred, I am!
   - Honestly, woman. You call yourself our mother.
   - [*to Fred*] Oh, I'm sorry, George.
   - I'm only joking, I am Fred!

6. - You wanna know the *real* difference between us?
   - Let me see . . . I know how to fence and you don't . . .
     Or I have class and you don't. Take your pick.
   - Why, I oughta!

---

[10] 1. D., 2. B., 3. F., 4. C., 5. A., 6. E.

Grandparents

Grandparents: A couple of old farts who have decided to give you the unconditional love they quite obviously withheld from your parents.
—JAMES NAPOLI

GROWING UP, I LOVED going to my grandparents's house. It always meant great things—money, toys, food, unconditional love . . . and all for the low, low price of a few smothering hugs and a few too many kisses. And as I basked in the glow, it wasn't until later that I realized (or would have known had I looked over at them) that my parents were standing there, mouths agape, and wondering, "Who in the hell are these people?"

Because the two people that were lavishing all this affection over me were the same people who could crush my parents with one well-placed word or a withering glance . . . who knew all their secrets and secret weaknesses . . . who could tell stories that would make them want to hide under a rock somewhere. . . .

As I grew older, I saw firsthand that these were not the angelic little old people I first thought. I began to understand the barbs and snarks they would toss like live grenades at my folks . . . and it impressed me even more.

Here are a few of the classics.

You do not really understand something unless you can
explain it to your grandmother.
—PROVERB

++

A grandmother is a babysitter who watches the kids
instead of the television.
—ANONYMOUS

+++

I always give my grandkids a couple of quarters when they
go home. It's a bargain.
—GENE PERRET

++

Becoming a grandmother is wonderful. One moment you're
just a mother. The next you are all-wise and prehistoric.
—PAM BROWN

+++

My grandmother started walking five miles a day when she
was sixty. She's ninety-seven now, and we don't know
where the hell she is.
—ELLEN DEGENERES

••

They say genes skip generations. Maybe that's why
grandparents find their grandchildren so likable.
—JOAN MCINTOSH

•••

If I had known how wonderful it would be to
have grandchildren, I'd have had them first.
—LOIS WYSE

••

My grandkids believe I'm the oldest thing in the world.
And after two or three hours with them, I believe it, too.
—GENE PERRET

•••

My grandmother is over eighty and still doesn't need glasses.
Drinks right out of the bottle.
—HENNY YOUNGMAN

••

Elephants and grandchildren never forget.
—ANDY ROONEY

•••

I wish I had the energy that my grandchildren have—if only
for self-defense.
—GENE PERRET

••

Every generation revolts against its fathers and
makes friends with its grandfathers.
—LEWIS MUMFORD

•••

It's amazing how grandparents seem so young once you become one.
—ANONYMOUS

✦✦

Varicose veins are the result of an improper selection of grandparents.
—WILLIAM OSLER

✦✦✦

By the time the youngest children have learned to keep the house tidy, the oldest grandchildren are on hand to tear it to pieces.
—CHRISTOPHER MORLEY

✦✦

The reason grandchildren and grandparents get along so well is because they have a common enemy.
—ANONYMOUS

✦✦✦

The best babysitters, of course, are the baby's grandparents.
You feel completely comfortable entrusting your baby to
them for long periods, which is why most grandparents
flee to Florida.
—DAVE BARRY

••

If your baby is "beautiful and perfect, never cries or fusses,
sleeps on schedule and burps on demand, an angel all the
time" . . . you're the grandma.
—TERESA BLOOMINGDALE

•••

When grandparents enter the door, discipline flies out the
window.
—OGDEN NASH

••

My grandfather was the kind of man who could follow
someone into a revolving door and come out first.
—STEPHEN FRY

•••

Something magical happens when parents turns into grandparents. Their attitude changes from "money-doesn't-grow-on-trees" to spending it like it does.
—PAUL LINDEN

◆◆◆

I'm very proud of my gold pocket watch. My grandfather, on his deathbed, sold me this watch.
—WOODY ALLEN

◆◆

Never have children, only grandchildren.
—GORE VIDAL

◆◆◆

I love being a grandmother. It's great to finally be greeted by someone who's bald, drooling, and wearing a diaper who's not my date.
—JOAN RIVERS

◆◆

Match Game:[11]

Match the saying with who is most likely to have said it.
PARENT OR GRANDPARENT

~♦~

1. It's okay, it was old. My mother gave it to me before she died. I didn't need it anymore.
2. You look thin. Can I get you some ice cream?
3. Your father repeated second grade, too.
4. If you don't like what's on your plate, I can make you something else.
5. Go get my wallet, I have a surprise for you.
6. The tooth fairy stopped here as well. He left you ten dollars.
7. Turn the channel, I wasn't watching that anyway.
8. I'm planning on giving you the car when you're ready to drive.
9. I just filled all the candy jars. Help yourself.
10. If you stay over, we can spend tomorrow at the arcade.

---

[11] All are from the grandparent. The parent doesn't say anything, just shakes his head in disbelief.

~•~

A little boy asks his grandfather to make a frog noise. His grandfather tells him he doesn't want to. The child continues to nag and ask him to make the frog noise. Finally exasperated, he asks his grandson, "Why are you so intent on hearing me make a frog noise?"

"Because mommy says when you croak, we can go to Disney World."

~•~

A little boy and his grandfather are in the backyard when they find a worm. The little boy says to his granddad, "I'll bet you five dollars I can get that worm to go back in its hole." His grandfather says, "Okay, I'll take that bet." The boy goes in the house, gets a can of hairspray, sprays the worm until its stiff, and shoves it in the hole. His grandfather gives him the $5 and goes into the house. When he comes out, he gives the boy another $5.

"But Grandpa, you already paid me."

" Yes I know . . . that's from your grandmother."

~•~

Just about the time a woman thinks her work is done,
she becomes a grandmother.
—EDWARD H. DRESCHNACK

✦✦✦

Getting your grandmother a cell phone that sends emails
and takes pictures is a great way to confuse her three times
with just one gift.
—CRAIG KILBORN

✦✦

My grandparents gave me scratch and cough books when I
was growing up. Scene of the accident coloring books.
—RICHARD LEWIS

✦✦✦

My grandfather lived to 103-years-old. Every morning, he
would eat a raw onion and smoke a cigar. You know what his
dying words were? No one does, they couldn't get near the guy.
—JONATHAN KATZ

✦✦

My parents are in their late sixties, and they still have sex.
Because they want grandchildren.
—WENDY LIEBMAN

✦✦

I just saw my grandmother, probably for the last time.
She's not sick or anything, she just bores the hell out of me.
—A. WHITNEY BROWN

✦✦✦

My Nana, ninety-years-old and still driving . . . not with me,
that would be stupid.
—TIM ALLEN

✦✦

Grandchildren don't make a man feel old; it's the knowledge
that he's married to a grandmother.
—G. NORMAN COLLIE

✦✦✦

Grandchildren: The only people who can get more out of
you than the IRS.
—GENE PERRET

✦✦

One of life's greatest mysteries is how the boy who wasn't good enough to marry your daughter can be the father of the smartest grandchild in the world.
—ANONYMOUS

+++

The older generation thought nothing of getting up at five every morning—and the younger generation doesn't think much of it either.

—JOHN J. WELSH

++

There was no respect for youth when I was young, and now that I am old, there is no respect for age—I missed it coming and going.
—J. B. PRIESTLEY

+++

When the grandmothers of today hear the word "Chippendales," they don't necessarily think of chairs.
—JOAN KERR

+++

Match the Quote to the Movie: Grandparents Edition[12]

A. *Little Miss Sunshine*   C. *The 40 Year Old Virgin*
B. *The Bucket List*   D. *The Philadelphia Story*

~•~

1. I would sell my grandmother for a drink—and you know how I love my grandmother.
2. That's a good looking grandma! My grandma looks like Jack Palance.
3. We live, we die, and the wheels on the bus go round and round.
4. - Grandpa, am I pretty?
   - You are the most beautiful girl in the world.
   - You're just saying that.
   - No! I'm madly in love with you and it's not because of your brains or your personality.

---

[12]   1. D., 2. C., 3. B., 4. A.

In-Laws

If she'd leave us alone,/We'd have a happy home/Sent from down below/ Mother-in-Law. Mother-in-Law!
—ERNIE K-DOE'S *MOTHER-IN-LAW*

JUST RECENTLY, A POLL taken in the US said more than half the population of the United States is fond of their in-laws . . . astounding that you can get that many people lying to pollsters at one time, no?

Since time immemorial, in-laws (more pointedly, MOTHERS-IN-LAW), have been the subject of ridicule, angst, distress, anxiety, uneasiness, and disquiet. And *those* are from the people that actually like their spouse's folks.

More often than not, at least one or both of the set is a controlling, invasive, bossy, intrusive and, yes, snarky creature, waiting to pounce at the first sign of weakness . . . and/or blood.

What follows are many a classic take on the phenomenon known as the instant family, a family created from marriage. Snarkily.

Mother-In-Law: A woman who destroys her son-in-law's
peace of mind by giving him a piece of hers.
—ANONYMOUS

++

I haven't spoken to my mother-in-law for two years.
We haven't quarreled. I just don't like to interrupt her.
—LES DAWSON

+++

I bought my mother-in-law a chair for Christmas, but she
wouldn't plug it in.
—ANONYMOUS

++

I know a mother-in-law that sleeps with her glasses on,
the better to see her son-in-law suffer in her dreams.
—ERNEST COQUELIN

+++

The wife's mother said, "When you're dead, I'll dance on your grave." I said, "Good, I'm being buried at sea."
—LES DAWSON

♦♦

My mother-in-law had a pain beneath her left breast. Turned out to be a trick knee.
—PHYLLIS DILLER

♦♦♦

I told my mother-in-law that my house was her house, and she said, "Get the hell off my property."
—JOAN RIVERS

♦♦

I just got back from a pleasure trip: took my mother-in-law to the airport.
—HENNY YOUNGMAN

♦♦♦

Behind every successful man is a proud wife and a surprised mother-in-law.
—HUBERT H. HUMPHREY

◆◆

Adam was the luckiest man; he had no mother-in-law.
—MARK TWAIN

◆◆◆

My wife said, "Can my mother come down for the weekend?" So I said, "Why?" and she said, "Well, she's been up on the roof two weeks already."
—BOB MONKHOUSE

◆◆

Her mother was a cultivated woman . . . she was born
in a greenhouse.
—SPIKE MILLIGAN

~•~

*An elderly couple was celebrating their 50th
anniversary at a dinner party. The husband
stood up and started telling the story of his
dating habits in his youth. It seemed that
every time he brought home a girl to meet his
mother, his mother didn't like her. So, finally,
he started searching until he found a girl who
not only looked like his mother and acted like
his mother, she even sounded like his mother.
So he brought her home one night to have
dinner . . . his father hated her.*

~•~

Happiness is seeing your mother-in-law's face on the side
of a milk carton.
—ANONYMOUS

••

~+~

Two lifeguards are working together on a beach when they notice sharks circling a woman who has drifted out a little too far. One begins to get up to race to her rescue when the other lifeguard grabs his arm and holds him back.

The first lifeguard asks, "Why are you holding me back? We have to go save that woman!"

The other replies, "Don't worry. That woman is my mother-in-law."

"Are you trying to kill her?"

"Although the idea may be tempting, that is not my intent. Just watch."

With that, the sharks organize themselves beneath the woman, and ride her on their backs all the way to shore, safely depositing her.

"How did you know that would happen?" asked the first lifeguard.

"Professional courtesy."

~+~

I couldn't ask for a better mother-in-law, as much as
I'd like to.
—MARY LOU TERRY

✦✦✦

I want to send my father-in-law a gift. How do you wrap up
a saloon?
—HENNY YOUNGMAN

✦✦

I should, many a good day, have blown my brains out, but
for the recollection that it would have given pleasure to my
mother-in-law; and, even then, if I could have been certain to
haunt her—but I won't dwell upon these trifling
family matters.
—LORD BYRON

✦✦✦

Difference between law and in-law is you can justify yourself
before law but never before in-laws.
—ANONYMOUS

♦♦♦

Of all the peoples whom I have studied, from city dwellers
to cliff dwellers, I always find that at least 50 percent would
prefer to have at least one jungle between themselves and
their in-laws.
—MARGARET MEAD

♦♦

The mother-in-law frequently forgets that she was a
daughter-in-law.
—ANONYMOUS

♦♦♦

My mother-in-law broke up my marriage. One night,
my wife came home early and found us in bed together.
—LENNY BRUCE

+++

The awe and dread with which the untutored savage
contemplates his mother-in-law are amongst the most
familiar facts of anthropology.
—JAMES GEORGE FRAZER

++

English law prohibits a man from marrying his mother-in-
law. This is our idea of useless legislation.
—ANONYMOUS

+++

I can always tell when the mother-in-law's coming to stay;
the mice throw themselves on the traps.
—LES DAWSON

♦♦

Conscience is a mother-in-law whose visit never ends.
—H. L. MENCKEN

♦♦♦

Never rely on the glory of the morning nor the smiles of your
mother-in-law.
—JAPANESE PROVERB

♦♦

Match the Quote to the Movie: In-Laws Edition[13]

A. *The Proposal*   D. *The In-Laws*

B. *The Princess Bride*   E. *Monster-in-Law*

C. *Meet the Parents*

~✦~

1. - I mean, can you ever really trust another human being, Greg?

   - Sure, I think so.

   - No. The answer is you cannot.

2. - [*Taking a knitted blanket out of the cabinet*] If you get chilly tonight use this. It has special powers.

   - Oh. What kind of special powers?

   - I call it the baby maker.

   - Okay.

   [*to Andrew*]

   - Better be super careful with this.

3. - I'm sorry I called you the worst father in the world. I'm sure there're at least two or three guys who are worse.

   - Thank you, Jer.

4. - Marriage is a sacred union which must only be entered with the utmost care.

   - Weren't you married four times?

5. - What was that for?

   - Because you have always been so kind to me, and I won't be seeing you again since I'm killing myself once we reach the honeymoon suite.

   - Won't that be nice. She kissed me, ha, ha, ha!

---

[13]   1. C., 2. A., 3. D., 4. E., 5. B.

Family

Relations never lend one any money, and won't give one
credit, even for genius. They are sort of an aggravated form
of the public.
—OSCAR WILDE

NOTHING SETS OFF A great snark-fest like
when a family gets together. The ingredients are
all there, like a recipe in some ancient cookbook. Take one
part animosity, one part long-buried childhood angst, add
the broth of years of slights, toss in a handful of well-placed
barbs, mix in nostalgic stories you would prefer were washed
from everyone's consciousness, bake at 750 degrees in the
heat of petty rivalry and jealousy, allow to cool, and then
serve. Hmmm . . . tasty.

Family: A social unit where the father is concerned with
parking space, the children with outer space, and the mother
with closet space.
—EVAN ESAR

••

Relations are a tedious lot of people who don't know
how to live, or when to die.
—OSCAR WILDE

•••

Distant relatives are the best kind; the further the better.
—KIN HUBBARD

••

Having a family is like having a bowling alley installed
in your brain.
—MARTIN MULL

•••

Important families are like potatoes. The best parts are
underground.
—FRANCIS BACON

+++

Happiness is having a large, loving, caring, close-knit family
in another city.
—GEORGE BURNS

++

I come from a family where gravy is considered a beverage.
—ERMA BOMBECK

+++

If you don't believe in ghosts, you've never been to a
family reunion.
—ASHLEIGH BRILLIANT

++

My family is really boring. They have a coffee table book called "Pictures We Took Just to Use Up the Rest of the Film."
—PENELOPE LOMBARD

+++

He that has no fools, knaves, nor beggars in his family was begot by a flash of lightning.
—THOMAS FULLER

++

Heredity is a splendid phenomenon that relieves us of responsibility for our shortcomings.
—DOUG LARSON

+++

If you ever start feeling like you have the goofiest, craziest, most dysfunctional family in the world, all you have to do is go to a state fair . . . because five minutes at the fair, you'll be going, "You know, we're alright."
—ANONYMOUS

++

When I can no longer bear to think of the victims of broken homes, I begin to think of the victims of intact ones.
—PETER DE VRIES

++

Blood may be thicker than water but it is still sticky, unpleasant, and generally nauseating.
—JANEANE GAROFALO

+++

I come from the typical American family. Me, my mother, her third husband, his daughter from a second marriage, my stepsister, her illegitimate son.
—CAROL HENRY

++

My parents only had one argument in forty-three years of marriage. It lasted forty-three years.
—CATHY LADMAN

+++

First 10 Year Anniversary Gifts:

1. Paper   What That Means To Her: Gift Certificate for spa treatments
           What That Means To Him: Paper for her printer

2. Cotton   What That Means To Her: 410 thread count 100% Egyptian cotton bedsheets
            What That Means To Him: Panties from Wal-Mart

3. Leather   What That Means To Her: Henri Bendel alligator satchel
             What That Means To Him: Red faux leather wallet from the Walgreens rack

4. Flowers   What That Means To Her: Bouquet of long stemmed American Beauty roses
             What That Means To Him: Flowers from the produce department of the IGA
             (Have to stop to pick up beer anyway.)

5. Wood   What That Means To Her: Antique cherry wood vanity
          What That Means To Him: Well, "wood," especially when she wears that hot little pink teddy

First 10 Year Anniversary Gifts:

6. Candy   What That Means To Her: Belgian chocolate
            What That Means To Him: Whitman
            Sampler
7. Wool   What That Means To Her: Cashmere
            What That Means To Him: Hunting socks
8. Linens   What That Means To Her: Lace tablecloth
            with matching napkins and table runner
            What That Means To Him: Absolutely
            nothing
9. Pottery What That Means To Her: An antique
            Chinese tea set
            What That Means To Him: A bong
10. Diamond What That Means To Her: You know
            What That Means To Him: Baseball tickets

A man with a hump-backed uncle mustn't make fun of another man's cross-eyed aunt.
—MARK TWAIN

••

The great advantage of living in a large family is that early lesson of life's essential unfairness.
—NANCY MITFORD

•••

Your basic extended family today includes your ex-husband or ex-wife, your ex's new mate, your new mate, possibly your new mate's ex, and any new mate that your new mate's ex has acquired.
—DELIA EPHRON

••

Family love is messy, clinging, and of an annoying and repetitive pattern, like bad wallpaper.
—FRIEDRICH NIETZSCHE

•••

Family is just accident. . . . They don't mean to get on your nerves. They don't even mean to be your family, they just are.
—MARSHA NORMAN

◆◆

Children in a family are like flowers in a bouquet: There's always one determined to face in an opposite direction from the way the arranger desires.
—MARCELENE COX

◆◆◆

If you cannot get rid of the family skeleton, you may at least make it dance.
—GEORGE BERNARD SHAW

◆◆

Parents often talk about the younger generation as if they didn't have anything to do with it.
—HAIM GINOTT

◆◆◆

When women feel they have learned to forgive their
mothers—and men, their fathers—all it usually means is
that they've decided to allow themselves the
same kind of behavior.
—MIGNON McLAUGHLIN

••

First we are children to our parents, then parents to
our children, then parents to our parents, then children to
our children.
—MILTON GREENBLATT

•••

When our relatives are at home, we have to think of all their
good points or it would be impossible to endure them.
—GEORGE BERNARD SHAW

••

My parents stayed together for forty-seven years—but that
was out of spite.
—WOODY ALLEN

•••

The family. We were a strange little band of characters
trudging through life sharing diseases and toothpaste,
coveting one another's desserts, hiding shampoo, borrowing
money, locking each other out of our rooms, inflicting pain
and kissing to heal it in the same instant, loving, laughing,
defending, and trying to figure out the common thread that
bound us all together.
—ERMA BOMBECK

✦✦✦

Women gather together to wear silly hats, eat dainty food,
and forget how unresponsive their husbands are. Men gather
to talk sports, eat heavy food, and forget how demanding
their wives are. Only where children gather is there any real
chance of fun.
—MIGNON McLAUGHLIN

✦✦

Several years before birth, advertise for a couple of parents
belonging to long-lived families.
—OLIVER WENDELL HOLMES

✦✦✦

Family life got better and we got our car back—as soon as
we put "I love mom" on the license plate.
—ERMA BOMBECK

••

Before most people start boasting about their family tree,
they usually do a good pruning job.
—O. A. BATTISTA

••

The other night, I ate at a really nice family restaurant.
Every table had an argument going.
—GEORGE CARLIN

••

Match the Quote to the Movie: Family Edition[14]

A. *Juno*   D. *Groundhog Day*
B. *The Lion King*   E. *Mean Girls*
C. *Four Christmases*

~+~

1. - You lie to your family at Christmas time?
   - Well, you can't really spell families without the lies . . .

2. It's the same thing your whole life . . . clean up your room, stand up straight, pick up your feet, take it like a man, be nice to your sister, don't mix beer and wine, ever . . . oh yeah, don't drive on the railroad tracks . . .

3. - You should look at adoption ads; I see them all the time in the Penny Saver . . .
   - They have ads for parents?
   - Yeah, desperately seeking spawn, right next to, like, terriers, and iguanas, and used fitness equipment and stuff.

4. - Where's Cady?
   - She went out.
   - She's grounded.
   - [*Surprised*] Are they not suppose to be let out when they're grounded?

5. - Is that a challenge?
   - Temper, temper. I wouldn't *dream* of challenging you.
   - Pity! Why not?
   - Well, as far as brains go, I got the lion's share. But, when it comes to brute strength . . . I'm afraid I'm at the shallow end of the gene pool.

---

[14]   1. C., 2. D., 3. A., 4. E., 5. B.

Conclusion

OKAY. THE GROUND FEELS a bit sturdier now.

Let's face it . . . we've all been through it:

Meddling mothers

Absent-minded grandfathers

Domineering fathers

Doting grandmothers

Evil and overbearing mothers-in-law

Noisy sisters

Intimidating fathers-in-law

Nauseating brothers

Goofy relatives

We've gone to onerous holiday dinners and get-togethers that make *Who's Afraid of Virginia Woolf?* look like *The Sound of Music*. We've attended depressing reunions, insipid recitals, dull weddings and bar mitzvahs, church socials, corny Sweet 16 parties/birthday parties/engagement parties . . . every manner of banal gathering. You name it, the family has made you attend at least one . . . hell, probably many of these "get-togethers."

All ripe targets for snark. Snark as a coping method . . . snark as a way to deal. . . . In the face of judgmental relatives, needy kids, countless guilt trips, bickering, pettiness, blowups, disputes, fistfights, and brawls, you'd go crazy without a little snark.

It's all in here. At the end of the day, just the knowledge that you're not alone can be a great source of solace. But like I said earlier . . . proceed with caution. They know your secrets, they know which buttons to push, and they know the ways to bring you to your knees.

Fight back!

In the end, they'll probably forgive you . . . until the next time.

Nah.

Acknowledgments

THE AUTHOR—FATHER, GRANDFATHER, SON, brother, uncle—wishes to thank the many family members that formed him. . . . And assure them he is being well cared for here in the asylum.

Oops, shock therapy time again . . .

A special thanks to mom for her unconditional love . . .

And, as always, my eternal love and thanks to RP, my rock and savior.

Stay snarky.

—Lawrence Dorfman

Index

The Snark Handbook

A Reference Guide to Verbal Sparring
by Lawrence Dorfman

It's impossible to go a full day without using snark, so why fight it? Snark is everywhere, from television to movies to everyday life. This lively collection provides hours of entertainment—better than an Etch A Sketch, and more fun than Silly Putty! At the heart of it, being in a state of snark can be one of the most useful tools at one's disposal and hence (yes, I used "hence"), a powerful way to get what you want. With snark, you can catch people completely off guard, and royally piss them off.

Included here is the Snark Hall of Fame, the Best Snarky Responses to Everyday Dumbassness, and much more. It's a book that will make you laugh. It's a book that will make someone else cry. It's a book every student of the American psyche (that's all of us, Sparky) needs to have. Let loose. Let your inner anger become a positive rather than a negative, but most of all, have fun. (Yeah, like that's something you know how to do.)

$12.95 Paperback • ISBN 978-1-60239-760-6

ALSO AVAILABLE

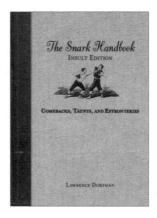

The Snark Handbook: Insult Edition

Comebacks, Taunts, and Effronteries
by Lawrence Dorfman

Author Lawrence Dorfman claims: "I love it when someone insults me. That means that I don't have to be nice anymore." In this latest incarnation of his bestselling series, Dorfman is in delicious form, dishing it out without any real consequences. The sharp-witted buyer (and that's you, my friend) may be wondering right about now: "Hey, how is this book any different from the first? That was full of insults, too." Yes, but these insults are different, and the author's retorts and taunts are so much more vitriolic than in the previous book.

Readers will find more material to actually use in day-to-day life, including streamlined instructions on when and how to mock your peers; how to use retorts with your spouse and children; and how our late, great ancestors used insults throughout history. This is not a mere collection of quotations. Dorfman speaks directly to his audience, serving as teacher, ringleader, and historian.

$12.95 Paperback • ISBN 978-1-61608-059-4

The Snark Handbook: Sex Edition

Innuendo, Irony, and Ill-Advised Insults on Intimacy
by Lawrence Dorfman

According to NewYorker.com, "Lawrence Dorfman assembled a heroic collection. I spent an hour in a state of catharsis, reveling in the sufficiency of the insults," in his previous homage to snarkdom (*Insult Edition*). Now just imagine the reviewer's state after an hour reading the *Sex Edition*. Here are sharply witty personal observations, jokes, quotations, he-said-she-said snarks, and much more. A taste of what's to come:

- "I'd like to meet the man who invented sex and see what he's working on now." —George Carlin

- "We have reason to believe that man first walked upright to free his hands for masturbation." —Lily Tomlin

- "Bigamy is having one husband or wife too many. Monogamy is the same." —Oscar Wilde

$12.95 Paperback • ISBN 978-1-61608-423-3